Marketing Mix

not 4Ps but fit for a competitive world

Books by Geoffrey Darnton

The Bomb and the Law

Information in the Enterprise:
it's more than Technology
(with Sergio Giacoletto)

Business Process Analysis

Emotional Abuse in the Classroom

Nuclear Weapons and International Lw

TPNW
Treaty on the Prohibition of Nuclear Weapons

Marketing Mix
not 4Ps but fit for a competitive world

plus chapters or parts in other books

Marketing Mix

not 4Ps but fit for a competitive world

Geoffrey Darnton

Requirements
Analytics
correctness•consistency•completeness

First edition published 2022
978-1-909231-12-2 (Paperback)
978-1-909231-13-9 (Hardback)
978-1-909231-14-6 (eBook)

Contents

Preface

Chapter 1
Introduction

Chapter 2
Origin of the Term 'Marketing Mix'

Chapter 3
Culliton

Chapter 4
McCarthy's 4Ps

Chapter 5

Positioning

Chapter 6

Beyond the Ps

Chapter 7

Full Circle

Chapter 8

Marketing Mix for Ideas

Chapter 9

Marketing Mix for Competition

Chapter 10

Marketing and Information Warfare

Chapter 11

Green Marketing Mix

Chapter 12

Conclusions and Recommendations

Appendix A

Check List of Marketing Considerations

Appendix B

Facsimile of 16th Century 'Marketing'

References

Index

Preface

Motivation for the book

This book is critical of a common practice among teachers, textbook writers, and students to approach questions about marketing mix with a bland, uncritical use of McCarthy's 4Ps, often accompanied by an additional problem of applying 4Ps to a company, not identifying a particular product, service, or idea for the analysis.

The problem is often compounded in textbooks that refer to marketing mix by simply stating headings for the 4Ps and not even identifying the origin or even including McCarthy in the list of references with appropriate citations in the text. This can apply to many courses. The net result is that many students may not have any idea at all that the 4Ps are associated primarily with McCarthy (1960).

Another problem arose while creating the text for this little book. It took around two years to assemble hardcopies of the sources to be sure that original copies were used. This required obtaining second-hand copies for books and papers that were already out of print. Unexpectedly, several of the original copies obtained on the second-hand market were books or papers that had been withdrawn and sold by university and college libraries. This means that academics and students in those institutions will be unable to access easily original copies of some key sources.

The origins of marketing and marketing mix are

explored, with emphasis on the early evolution of thinking about marketing mix.

Positioning, although not claimed to be part of marketing mix is included in the analysis along with a suggestion that when constructing a marketing mix, positioning should be considered for inclusion. There is brief mention of emerging alternative approaches to marketing mix, such as Cs, Vs, As, and Os.

The book explains that the approaches to marketing mix which have emerged in the past 70 years or so, when all the approaches are unpacked, result in a number of candidate marketing mix elements. This means that the fundamental problem identified in research from the 1920s onwards remains unresolved – and the conscientious creator of a marketing mix remains a 'mixer of ingredients'.

The book suggests, and provides examples, that the most appropriate way to create a marketing mix is to identify what features of a product, service, or idea are particularly important to final and intermediate buyers, consumers, or users and a marketing mix should be constructed from those features – even if they don't have a 'P', 'C', 'A' or 'V' as an initial letter.

The book concludes with recommendations for the teacher, text book writer, practitioner, and student what to consider when creating a marketing mix.

Essentially, return to the origins of marketing mix with stronger focus on the needs and wants of buyers, consumers, and users.

This is a conceptual book, not an empirical book.

Discussions about marketing mix is traditionally associated with the marketing of products and services.

One of the author's research interests is information warfare. Over the years he has become increasingly convinced that marketing can be considered to be a branch of information warfare. The route to this conclusion is via the idea of positioning because both positioning and information warfare are concerned with affecting the minds of people who are exposed to the ideas being promoted by the marketing or information warfare. This is a theme that will be developed further in another book. As can be seen below, the two principal writers about positioning are very close to this conclusion also.

The modern world is now intensively competitive. Increasingly, sellers find that the greatest problem they face is shifting from customer wants and needs to dealing with the competitive environment. This little book is radical in its initial rejection of simple 4Ps approaches to marketing mix and replacing them with elements based on customer wants and needs and addressing a modern competitive environment.

Over the past hundred years marketing has progressed from being production oriented through being customer oriented to today's need to be competitor oriented. Marketing mix elements are suggested for ideas and competition.

Geoffrey Darnton
Bournemouth
March 2022

Acknowledgements

I would like to thank Al Ries, Laura Ries, and Jack Trout for their assistance to obtain copies of their papers. Thanks are also due to Michelle Heller, Emma Korpe, Cecile Landswerk and Sarah von Rueti for agreeing that their work can be referenced, havimg been made available to the author originally for an academic purpose.

Chapter 1

Introduction

Introductory Comments

When did people start to use the term 'marketing'? The answer is probably lost in antiquity, but there is an intriguing example from the 16th century. That appears in an English translation of Calvin's seminal work (1561) that set out substantial contributions to the emerging Protestant branch of Christianity. He was talking about marketing by the Roman Catholic Church: "...how filthy markettinges they vse, how vnhonest gaynes thei make wt their massings, with how great raucning they fill their coveteousnes." (Norton, 1574; book 4, chapter 18, para. 18 – see Annex 2). Comments like that would not endear Calvin to the Catholic Church! The same work has multiple uses of the term 'market'. However, the fact of the term 'marketing' being used in 1561 raises the question whether it has been used earlier or not. The Oxford English Dictionary has the same 1561 source as its earliest example of using the term (OED, 2009). That is a challenge for literature review archaeologists! Until an earlier use can be identified, the origin of 'marketing' is that Calvin-Norton combination resulting in that work in English. Until new information is discovered, we need to roll forward almost 400 years to understand the origins of the term 'marketing mix' in the 20th century.

This book is not concerned with all approaches to marketing mix which have emerged during the 20th and 21st centuries; it is focused on the early development, along with associated reflections. It looks at the emergence of the term itself, followed by a discussion of early key writers who have contributed to the discussion. Many writers have looked at more recent marketing mix formulations, such as Allison (2013).

This book has also been inspired by the many students over the years who have approached questions about marketing mix simply by diving straight into an answer based on a 4Ps marketing mix using McCarthy's model, without any introduction or critical analysis and evaluation of the concepts of marketing mix or those 4Ps. Indeed, many students (and some textbooks) use 4Ps without even identifying the key source as McCarthy. As a secondary matter, the author has also seen hundreds of students proceeding to present a marketing mix for a company rather than a product. What has shocked him even more than this, is the number of his students who have done this after lectures and classes about the evolution of marketing mix which include many key authors and variants easily available to the diligent student who bothers to look and research.

This all raises two important issues. Firstly, what is it about those students who dive straight in to a 4Ps marketing mix notwithstanding a great deal of material out there to support a much more critical discussion? Secondly, is that very common phenomenon of using only a 4Ps marketing mix reasonable and justifiable?

The author has also been worried by some recent textbooks that have marketing themes but also only present a 4Ps marketing mix. Maybe the students can be forgiven to some extent for merely replicating what they have found in those textbooks or been taught in classes. The author does not understand how the authors of those textbooks (they will not be name and shame in this book) can take such a sloppy approach to such an important topic.

Exasperation at the number of students, textbooks and courses that present marketing mix blandly as '4Ps' inspired the author to look further into this phenomenon and revisit the early evolution of marketing mix.

Early on in the author's investigations, he discovered that his research was not going to be as easy as expected originally – he needed to delve into academic literature archaeology! Simply obtaining copies of the relevant original works proved to be much more difficult than anticipated. To a great extent, that is because so many university libraries have withdrawn and sold copies of earlier original works. Presumably that is because someone looked at the date and thought 'too old'. This poses a real challenge for any academic who wants to check original sources and do some critical thinking (critical thinking is the term used a lot by academics in English, but the word 'comparative' is probably more appropriate than 'critical'). As will be demonstrated shortly, some writers, and certainly some writers of more modern textbooks, really need to take a more careful look at what some of those early authors actually said – many comments in later papers and books simply demonstrate that those writers did not access the original works.

4

This book starts by tracing the origins of "marketing mix" and a more detailed look at McCarthy's 4Ps, demonstrating that so many textbooks and courses have not even understood the key points McCarthy made. The book goes on to discuss positioning, suggesting that although it is not part of the original 4Ps, it should be addressed by anyone producing a marketing mix. Writers and research earlier than McCarthy are explored and the book comes full circle back to a set of recommendations. Simple examples of alternative marketing mixes are included.

Origin of the Term 'Marketing Mix'

Early Industrial Activity and Research (1920s on)

Up to the late 1940s, there was a great deal of practical industrial and commercial marketing activity, which, as can be expected, was accompanied by a substantial academic effort to find patterns and frameworks to make sense of all the industrial and commercial marketing activity.

Academic activity was focused for a long time to try to identify if there is any general pattern to the proportion of costs needed to get goods to market and the final consumer. For example, Borden (1964) reports a study by the Harvard Bureau of Business Research (part of Harvard University) of a cost study of food manufacturers in 1929.

Culliton's 'Mixer of Ingredients'

Borden commented that there were so many different ways to do marketing. He summe up the fundamental 'research question' as:

> "What combination of marketing procedures and policies has been or might be adopted to bring about desired behaviours of trade and consumers at costs that will permit a profit? (Borden, 1964; p8).

Specifically, how can advertising, personal selling, pricing, packaging, channels, warehousing, and the other elements of a marketing program be manipulated and fitted together in a way that will give a profitable operation?"

So, where did the term 'marketing mix' come from? Is it clear where the idea comes from? After some literature archaeology it is not difficult to identify the origins of the term (the origin is much clearer than the mystery of who first started to use the term 'SWOT' – which is still clouded in obscurity, or who was first to use the term 'marketing'). If marketing mix is interpreted as 4Ps – the answer is McCarthy (1960). However, the term pre-dates McCarthy.

The fundamental research question that troubled many researchers at Harvard University (and other universities) from at least the 1920s onwards concerned what activities and at what costs need to be performed to bring products and services to market successfully? Researchers were looking for a 'silver bullet' of marketing. Despite decades of research, this 'silver bullet' remained elusive in the late 1940s (today, it remains elusive!).

In 1948, a fascinating little book was published by the Harvard Business School (Culliton, 1948). A key fascination about the book, is that it was a report about research project failure, rather than success:

> "Discovery of the fact that I could not find what I had started out to seek — useful figure data on what manufacturers spent for marketing — made the preparation of this book disturbing", (Culliton, 1948; vii).

This possible complex combination was summed up by Culliton (1948) who described the business executive responsible for marketing as "…the business executive is described in this book as a "decider", an "artist" — a "mixer of ingredients" who sometimes follows a recipe prepared by others, sometimes prepares his own recipe as he goes along, sometimes adapts a recipe to the ingredients immediately available, and sometimes experiments with or invents ingredients no one else has tried. In this spirit, frequent use is made of such analogies as "pattern of costs", "recipe", "mix", "ingredient", and the like." – Thus we have the "mix" and the "mixer of ingredients" (Culliton, 1948; pp5-6). Culliton's book has a detailed discussion of the factors examined by the Harvard researches of the time, and even though written in 1948, would be today an excellent book for study by MBA students and managers who would like to know many of the areas of decisions which will challenge them.

Borden - originator of term 'Marketing Mix'

Borden asserts: the "phrase "marketing mix", which I began to use in my teaching and writing some 15 years ago" (Borden, 1964; p386). As Borden was writing in 1964, he is claiming to have used the term "marketing mix" from around 1949, just after Culliton's book. Indeed, prior to McCarthy's 1960 book, Borden (1950) wrote: "One of the main tasks in many of the cases in this volume is to determine suitable marketing mixes for particular situations, with advertising as the focal point in our considerations" (p16) (note that 'advertising' does not start with a P!). In the same book, Borden uses the term 'marketing mix' in several other places (p157; p160; pp164-6; p380; …). Subsequently, Borden and Marshall (1959) have an Exhibit 1 – The Concept of the Marketing Mix (ibid, pp23-4). Borden and Marshall explicitly attribute the term "marketing mix" to Culliton (ibid, fn1 p23). One point to note about this, is that when looking for the origin of the term 'marketing mix', students (and many academics) have frequently found reference to Borden (1964), whereas a more accurate source for an original use of the term in a book is Borden (1950). All the examples provided by Borden and Marshall are focused on the primary topic of their books, which is advertising.

At this point, it is useful to give examples of what kinds of 'mix' Borden is talking about, because 4Ps are not intuitive:

> "...the product characteristics, or form to adopt,
> the prices to charge, the channels of distribution
> to use, and the selling methods to use, in turn have
> a bearing on the forms of advertising to use..."
> (Borden, 1950; p16).

Borden and Marshall suggest: the behaviour of consumers; the behaviour of the trade; the behaviour of competition; the behaviour of government agencies; product planning; packaging; pricing; branding; channels of distribution; physical handling (warehousing, transportation); quantity and quality of personal selling; servicing; quantity and quality of the other tools of sales promotion; kind and quality of marketing-research information; quantity and quality of advertising, including display. (Borden and Marshall, 1959; pp23-4). These examples contain many factors that need to be taken into account when deciding how to plan the marketing of a product or service – the marketing mix. You will also see the germs of what eventually emerged as Porter's 5-forces in these examples.

The term 'Marketing Mix' is in the title of Frey's book (Frey, 1956) which unfortunately has no references or citations. As will be seen shortly, McCarthy developed Frey's ideas.

Chapter 3

Culliton

Culliton's Candidate Marketing Mix Elements

Culliton was involved extensively in the early research done at the Harvard University Business School to identify what costs and categories of costs were deployed by companies trying to bring products to market.

It was seen earlier that the list of possible ingredients for a marketing mix is considerable. The candidate marketing mix ingredients derived from Culliton's work is summarized here. Those who wish to create a marketing mix would do well to start with this list and continue with elements based on what customers are looking for when they want to buy or use a particular product, service, or idea.

Culliton's key contribution to the evolution of the term 'marketing mix' was to identify the business executive responsible for marketing as a 'mixer of ingredients'. He goes on to present an alphabetical list of those possible ingredients (which he calls 'Available Order-Getting Ingredients'): advertising; alertness to know when business is available; catalogues; channels of distribution; continuing relationships; credit rating; custom design; customer relationships;

demonstrations; display; entertainment; financial assistance to customers; getting the first order; glamour; guarantees; knowing the customer as an individual, not a statistic; leadership; licensing; none (some companies have no order-getting costs at all); packaging; performance specifications; personal selling; portion of the market; price; price adjustment; price quoting; product; product development and improvement; product family; quality/price balance; reciprocity; reputation; service; term contracts; tough job (skilled work force); widening the market (Culliton, 1948; pp 20-38). Culliton, without providing any data for backup, asserts this list has been constructed after visits to and discussions with several actual businesses, asking "what costs do you call marketing costs?". This is offered only as a list of possible ingredients for a 'mix' and only some would be selected in each case.

Chapter 4

McCarthy's 4Ps

McCarthy Introduces the 4Ps

In terms of marketing mix, the eras of pre-Culliton, Culliton, Borden and Frey, saw a lot of research about marketing costs, and what ingredients might be combined into a marketing mix.

The real 'game changer' for the term 'marketing mix' came in 1960 with McCarthy's book, *Basic Marketing* (McCarthy, 1960). In his chapter B1, Marketing Management and the Consumer, his extremely famous 4Ps are introduced in a section Development of a Marketing Mix.

Comsumers and Company Objectives are Essential

Those who strip away all of McCarthy's discussion and work with only those 4Ps should keep in mind the two opening sentences of that section:

> "The consumer is of overriding importance in the selection of a strategy. When the target consumers have been chosen, marketing management can combine all of the tools at its command in the effort to hit the target" (McCarthy, 1960; p 41).

Note carefully – until the target consumers along with company objectives have been identified, a marketing mix cannot be developed. McCarthy presents a simple diagram to show the 4Ps, consumers and company objectives. An adaptation of that is presented in Figure 1, to include company objectives (also identified by McCarthy as key).

McCarthy's book certainly talks about marketing mix; but he does not discuss the origin of the term – he merely uses it:

> "Marketing strategy and designing a marketing mix … are stressed to give the student the big picture…Based on consumer behaviour and company objectives, a marketing mix is developed next out of four ingredients, called the four P's: Product, Place (that is channels and institutions), Promotion, and Price…developing the "right" product and making it available at the "right" place with the "right" promotion, and at the "right" price, to satisfy target consumers and still meet the objectives of the business" (McCarthy, 1960; pp v-vi).

Although he has both Borden and Culliton in his index, the entries do not point to the relevant books necessary to understand the origin of marketing mix. This raises the intriguing question of whether McCarthy did not know about those books by Borden and Culliton, or he knew about them and decided not to include references to them. Although McCarthy does not discuss the origin of marketing mix, he is certainly aware of uses of the term prior to his book. For example, his book contains a Checklist of Marketing Considerations which he has adapted by arranging, according to the 4Ps, a checklist from a book by A.W. Frey (1956), *The Effective Marketing Mix*. McCarthy's adaptation is attached as Appendix A to this book, along with a brief commentary about the adaptation, in order to provide easy access to the kind of information students and practitioners should

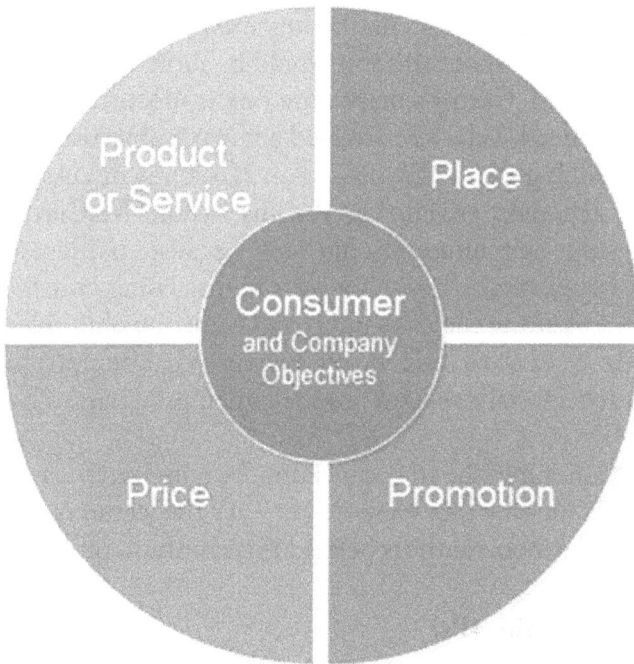

**Figure 1 Marketing Mix 4 Ps emphasizing their
focus on consumers**

(adapted from McCarthy, 1960; p45)

take into consideration when preparing a marketing mix. The index to McCarthy's 1960 book contains an entry for Frey, but not to McCarthy's most detailed use of Frey - therefore it is reasonable to conclude that the indexing of McCarthy's book was careless.

As Figure 1 shows, it is a mistake to think that when talking about marketing mix, McCarthy was only talking about 4Ps – it would be more accurate to say that McCarthy's marketing mix is 4Ps focused on a C. Indeed, as he also stressed company objectives, he was talking about 4Ps focused on 2Cs. Only discussing the 4Ps risks trivializing the discussion. McCarthy does not help himself in his book, because so often, in several places, he himself reverts to discussing only the 4Ps forgetting the consumers and company objectives.

It is easy to find many very trivial attempts by students to talk about a product when producing a list of 4Ps.

Sometimes the students cannot be criticized because that is the way they were taught – it's the lecturers and some textbook authors behind this common problem.

What are the 4Ps?

When McCarthy produced his 4Ps focused on 2Cs, the key words he used for the Ps, product, place, promotion, and price were only very brief and summary words including much more complex and detailed considerations. It is worthwhile recalling what he had in mind:

> "**Product** – In this section we will consider all of the problems of developing the product or service which the company chooses to offer to the target consumers. Services will be included as a type of product, although an

intangible one". Note the equality of service with product. This is a theme returned to later when discussing some of the later critiques of McCarthy (McCarthy, 1960; pp 45-6).

"**Place** – Within this category, the major problems are where, when, and by whom the goods and services are to be offered for sale. Wholesaling, retailing, transportation, storage, and financing are discussed. Under "place" will be considered all the problems, functions, and institutions involved in getting the right product to the target consumer" (McCarthy, 1960; p 47).

The list of elements included by McCarthy in his 'Place' includes complex matters such as channels of distribution and transportation. The word 'place' in this context is a massive over-simplification.

"…**Promotion** is concerned with any method which communicates to the target consumer about the right product which will be sold in the right place at the right price. In this category, all the problems of sales promotion, advertising, and the development, training and utilization of a sales force must be covered – that is, the development of the 'promotional mix'" (McCarthy, 1960; p 47).

Again, McCarthy is including many complex matters in another of his 4Ps.

"**Price** – After the marketing manager has developed plans for getting the right Product at the right Place, and planned to tell consumers about it with the right Promotion, he still must decide on the Price which will make this package attractive to consumers as well as profitable to the company. The price area will consider all of the problems of deciding whether to use price aggressively as a part of the marketing mix and if so, which price or prices. The nature of competition in the markets has some bearing on this problem, as do the existing trade practices, such as markups, discounts, and terms of sale. The problem of staying within the law with respect to price must be considered" (McCarthy, 1960; p 47).

Note the extensive range of matters included in the Price category.

"**Consumer** – In the center of the diagram, surrounded by the four P's, was a "C" for the consumer. The consumer is the focal point of all marketing efforts. For that matter, according to the marketing concept, the consumer should be the focal point for all business efforts. Within the Consumer area, factors bearing on consumer behaviour, characteristics, attitudes, or intentions will be considered. We will think of ultimate consumers (the man on the street), as well as intermediate consumers (people or institutions, such as retailers and wholesalers who buy for resale, and manufacturers who buy goods and services for use in making products destined for others). Our analysis of consumers will consider facts about them – their environment as well as their habits and motives- which may have a bearing on the relative importance of each of the four P's in the marketing mix" (McCarthy, 1960; pp 47-8).

"**Objectives** – Although the objectives may be set, it is extremely important that they be well defined, since they shape the direction and operation of the entire business. Marketing management is responsible for satisfying consumers in the light of these objectives" (McCarthy, 1960; p 49).

Company objectives are More that Just Profit

McCarthy continues his discussion of objectives pointing out it is too simplistic to consider only profit; there may be other objectives also.

It was decided for this book to include these extensive quotes from McCarthy about his 4Ps to convey the depth and complexity of a marketing mix. It has become very difficult for students and academics to have access to McCarthy's original 1960 book because so many university libraries have disposed of their copies. Hopefully, these more detailed quotes from McCarthy will provide sufficient detail for academics and students to know what McCarthy included in his 4Ps.

McCarthy's 4Ps are both a blessing and a curse.

They are a blessing in that they offer a very simplified set of elements to include in a marketing mix, when compared with the lists of elements from the pre-Culliton, Culliton, and Borden eras. However, note that if the McCarthy Ps are unpacked into a list of elements that should be included when constructing a McCarthy-type marketing mix, the number of elements to consider is no different from the lists produced by the generation prior to McCarthy. What McCarthy produced was an extremely simplistic set of four elements to bring together a very disparate set of more extensive elements.

Marketing Mix is for a Product, not a Company

4Ps are a curse because generations of teachers, students, and textbooks have stripped McCarthy's basic model of 4Ps focused on 2Cs down to only 4Ps. So, generations of students have been taught didactically that marketing mix is 4Ps. That is very easy to teach and examine students on. It is lazy teaching and learning *par excellence* devoid of critical thinking. It is even worse in that often those stripped down 4Ps have lost all the qualifications and nuances present in McCarthy's original work. Then, to complete the corrupt use of McCarthy's initial models, so often when a marketing mix is produced, it is done for a company without any consideration that the production of a marketing mix must be for a particular product, service, or idea, not a company.

McCarthy the beginning of PESTEL?

To McCarthy, the 4Ps were considered to be controllable factors for the marketing manager. Immediately after presenting his 4Ps he presents a set of uncontrollable factors: cultural and social environment; political and legal environment; economic environment; existing business structure; and, resources and objectives of the firm. Figure 1 is extended for these uncontrollable factors, and presented in Figure 2.

What is interesting about this diagram (Figure 2) is that the uncontrollable factors are almost PESTEL: Political, Economic, Social, Environmental, Legal; only the Technical or Technological is missing.

McCarthy's 4Ps after 1960

From 1960, McCarthy's book went through a series of editions (for example 2nd edition 1964, 3rd edition 1968).

The editions provide rearrangements and additional material but the fundamentals of his marketing mix remain the same. His 1964 book did provide an interesting clarification about marketing mix elements: "In the center of the diagram, surrounded by 4 Ps is a C for the customer. The customer is the focal point of all marketing efforts. For that matter, according to the marketing concept, the customer should be the focal point of all business efforts. But the customer is not a part of the marketing mix" (McCarthy, 1964; p40). Hence the focus of the 4Ps is the customer. What McCarthy was getting at, was that the marketing mix contains elements that can be controlled by

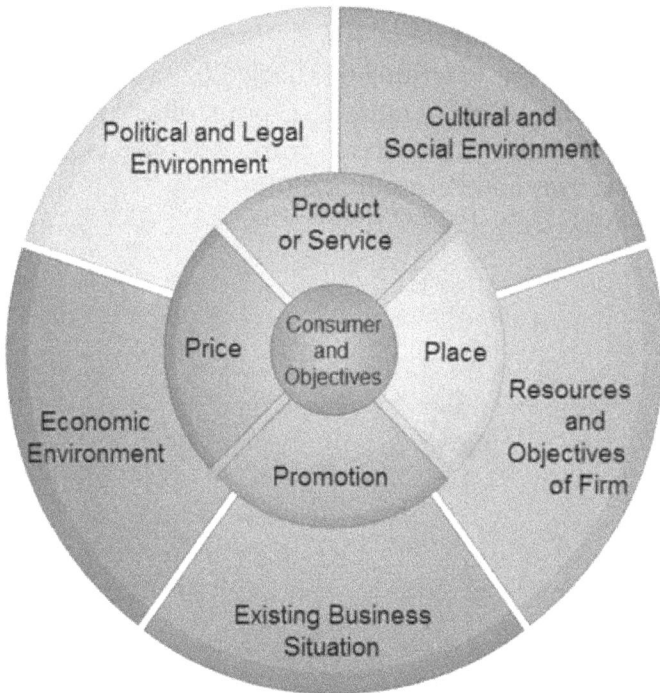

Figure 2 McCarthy's Controllable and Uncontrollable Factors

Adapted from McCarthy (1960) p49

managers. The other factors, the uncontrollable factors as identified in Figure 2, cannot be controlled by management. That does raise a moot point whether resources and objectives of the firm should really be considered to be uncontrollable elements, or whether they are properly part of marketing mix. Anyhow, whatever the moot points, McCarthy's view is that marketing mix is those 4Ps.

At the tine of writing this book (2022), McCarthy's marketing works continue in print, albeit with co-authors/editors in recent years; see, for example, McCarthy and Perreault (2000).

McCarthy, 1928-2015.

Chapter 5

Positioning

Introductory Comments

One enduring fact about McCarthy's 4Ps is that many people 'instinctively' think that even if the 4Ps are insufficient, additional marketing mix elements should also begin with a 'P'! Indeed, following McCarthy, other writers have attempted to create new Ps or pick another starting alphabet letter and have marketing mix elements that begin with the selected alternative letter (e.g. Cs or Vs).

That makes McCarthy's 4Ps a superb example of 'positioning' – not that positioning was one of McCarthy's Ps. In the minds of so many people, marketing mix is those 4Ps, or if it is something else, it should begin with a P.

Origins of Positioning in Marketing

Positioning, as a marketing concept, was introduced, in the 1960s – not long after McCarthy's 4Ps became firmly established in the marketer's mind.

The idea of Positioning in a marketing sense gained substantial traction following a 1969 article by Jack Trout. Trout puts it thus: "…consider the mind as a memory bank. Like a memory bank, the mind has a slot or "position" for each bit of information it has chosen to retain" (Trout, 1969). He goes on to explain that a mind does not retain every bit of information it comes across; it :

> "...accepts only that which matches prior knowledge or experience. In other words, the mind will accept only new information which fits its previous pattern of slots or positions".

Ayer's New Product Model and Positioning

Trout was not the only person to use positioning around that time (mid- to late-1960s). The idea of product positioning was used in what is known as Ayer's New Product Model. Product positioning (PP) is one of the factors used to estimate advertising recall. The data used in the Ayer's model was collected between mid-1965 and early 1968 (Claycamp and Liddy, 1969; p 415) There is a detailed discussion of the model in the Claycamp and Liddy paper. An interesting commentary on the Ayer model is available in Midgley (1977; pp 255-258) while comparing several models.

Simple Illustration of Positioning

The author has found that a simple exercise run with students a few times, helps them to grasp the significance of positioning quickly:

> "Author to a student: "if money is not an issue, what car would you like to buy?";
> Student: "a Lamborghini".
> Author: "Do you have a Lamborghini in your family?".
> Student: "No".
> Author: "Have you ever driven or had a ride in a

Lamborghini?".
Student: "No".
Author: "Do you have any friends who own or have experienced a Lamborghini?".
Student: "No".
Author: "So, let's understand this – you would like a car you have never experienced and none of your family or friends has experienced either?".
Student: "Yes, I would just like one".
Author: "So, somehow, Lamborghini have managed to get into your head so that you would like one; that is an example of positioning".

Of course, on occasions this little exercise has failed because the Author tried it on a student who has experienced a Lamborghini!

Ries and Trout

Trout continues with further discussion and examples of positioning. His 1969 article was followed in 1972 by a series of 3 further articles with Ries (Ries and Trout, 1972a, 1972b, 1972c). Those three articles essentially develop and give more examples of the themes set out in Trout's 1969 article. Towards the end of 1972 there was an interesting article in the Wall Street Journal about the significance of positioning, providing further examples and commentary (Kwitny, 1972). Ries and Trout's first book appeared in 1981 (Ries and Trout, 1981). The book adds further detail and case studies to themes developed in the 1969 and 1972 articles.

Add Positioning to Marketing Mix?

Positioning begins with a P. It is radically different from McCarthy's 4Ps. I strongly advise that it is added to the list of marketing mix Ps. Thus we would have 5Ps (see Figure 3). Apart from Product, which identifies which product or service is the subject of the marketing mix, positioning may well be the most important because it is focused on how customers think about the product, service or idea.

Positioning can be applied to Companies

Positioning goes beyond specific products, services or ideas because it can be applied to companies and brands – what 'position' the company or brand has in the minds of people. Ries and Trout view positioning as a way to communicate in an over-communicated world. In the UK do Aldi and Lidl worry if they are positioned in the minds of shoppers as relatively cheap supermarkets? – no, because that is where they want to be positioned in the minds of shoppers.

It should be noted that Ries and Trout offer no critique of McCarthy or Borden and make no suggestion that Positioning should be included or added to marketing mix based on Ps.

Positioning does not seem to have achieved the same academic traction as McCarthy's 4Ps. That is not surprising because in all their writings, Ries and Trout do not play any academic game. Their works are completely devoid of any references to sources other than their own papers. Notwithstanding that, positioning has gained considerable practitioner traction, and should be considered by academics along with McCarthy's 4Ps. Comparing positioning and McCarthy's 4Ps should be very fertile ground for critical thinking by teachers text book writers and students.

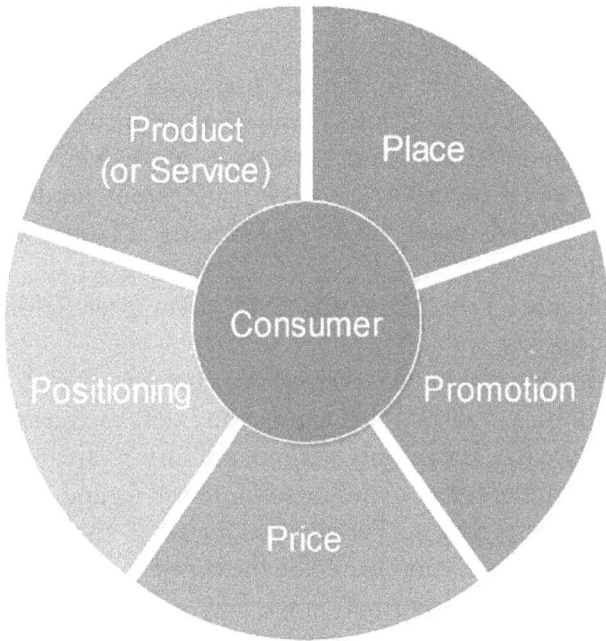

Figure 3 - Marketing Mix 5Ps after adding Positioning

Hence the earlier comment that McCarthy's 4Ps constitute an excellent example of positioning in Ries and Trout terms because many students and marketing writers are resistant to going beyond 4Ps when they discuss marketing mix.

As a footnote to the discussion of Ries, Trout, and positioning, it is worth noting some subsequent work. In 1986, Ries and Trout wrote about Marketing Warfare (Ries and Trout, 1986), and Trout produced an updated book about positioning (Trout with Rivkin, 1996).

Figure 3 - Marketing Mix 5Ps after adding Positioning

The book about Marketing Warfare uses an analogy of military strategy, dedicating the book to Karl von Clausewitz. They apply various military strategies to corporate conduct giving many interesting and useful examples as they go. Perhaps a more useful analogy for future consideration would be the connection between marketing and information warfare.

Trout's 1996 book expands on earlier work about positioning, and gives some new examples. It is moving towards more academic respectability because it does have more quotations by a variety of people. What is missing are the citations and references to track them back.

Chapter 6

Beyond the Ps

Beyond the 4Ps and 5Ps

McCarthy's 4Ps have endured until now. The first major proposal for modification which gained traction was by Booms and Bitner (1981). Their paper is not an empirical paper; it is purely conceptual. They only offer prescription for changes, and provide no examples of the application of their proposed additional Ps:

> "…the service marketing mix should be expanded to include 3 new P's" (Booms and Bitner, 1981; p48).

> "**Participants** – All human actors who play a part in service delivery and thus influence the buyer's perception: namely, the firm's personnel and other customers in the service environment.
> **Physical evidence** – The environment in which the service is assembled and where the firm and customer interact; and any tangible commodities which facilitate performance or communication of the service.
> **Process of Service Assembly** – The actual procedures, mechanisms, and flow of activities by which the service is delivered." (Booms and Bitner, 1981; p 48

Booms and Bitner attribute Participants to Shostack 1977a, and Physical evidence to Shostack 1977b).

This provides an additional 3Ps, so that many writers and students refer to the 4Ps being extended to

7Ps. Rather than the extension by Booms and Bitner, it may be more appropriate to refer to Booms, Bitner, and Shostack to provide a more academically accurate attribution.

This is in stark contrast to the work of Ries and Trout who provide extensive examples of positioning, but no citations and references.

Thus, if we have McCarthy's 4Ps extended by Booms and Bitner the result is 4Ps to 7Ps. If Ries and Trout's positioning is added, we have 4Ps to 5Ps to 8Ps (see Figure 4).

Other writers have proposed additional Ps for marketing mix, for example Lawrence et al. (1998) who propose more Ps for the internet age (Paradox, Perspective, Paradigm, Persuasion, and Passion).

Beyond All Ps

It had to happen: McCarthy, supplemented by Booms and Bitner, became so deeply positioned in the mind of teachers, textbook writers, and students as the meaning of 'marketing mix', that some writers had to tackle the Ps head on and try to replace that positioning of the Ps. If those writers had read the comments in the Ries and Trout book about marketing warfare (Ries and Trout, 1986) they would have realized that the likelihood of replacing the positioning of marketing mix as Ps by something else was very low. Some writers decided to suggest replacing the Ps with a different set of elements starting with a letter other than P, but all elements starting with the same alternative letter.

One example of moving away from 4Ps can be found in the work of Shimizu (n.d.). He proposes a 7Cs compass model that encompasses a 4Cs model.

His 7Cs are:

(C1) Corporation and C-O-S (where C-O-S is competitor, organization, Stakeholder); (C2) Commodity; (C3) Cost; (C4) Communication; (C5) Channel; (C6) Consumer; (C7) Circumstances

It is not necessary to repeat information about these Cs as the original paper is easily available. Identifying the dates of these proposals is not so simple. Some writers and websites give dates of 1973 and 1979 for various elements in the 7Cs Compass Model, but these remain unverified at the time of writing this book.

A further early example of this, is Lauterborn (1990) who suggested replacing the 4Ps with 4Cs:

"It's time to retire McCarthy's Famous Four P's, the Rosetta Stone of marketing education for 20 years ... It's time for a new formula: Lauterborn's Four C's".

Consumer wants and needs – You can't sell whatever you can make any more. (forget product).

Cost to satisfy – that want or need. (forget price).

Convenience to buy – People don't have to go anyplace anymore (forget place).

Communication – from the buyer (forget promotion).

What Lauterborn is doing, is re-emphasizing a key point made by McCarthy in 1960 that the 4Ps are focused on the C in the middle – the consumer – and adding some elaboration. The points made by Lauterborn will certainly help the marketer. The points should also be picked up by teachers, textbook writers, and students who should all be presenting a much more critical discussion of marketing mix, than merely presenting an uncritical 4Ps. Another 7Cs marketing mix is suggested by Dennis et al. (2005).

Following Lauterborn, there have been further

suggestions for different combinations of marketing mix elements. Examples include Bhatia (2010) who suggests Vs, and White (2013) who suggests adding Os and As.

Summary of Early Marketing Mix Ideas

This book has started from Culliton and passed through McCarthy, Trout, Ries, Booms and Bitner, Shimizu, Lauterborn and several other authors who have proliferated more ideas about what can go into a marketing mix. This early history is summarized in Figure 5.

See the following chapter for ideas about marketing mix focussed on customer wants, not 4Ps.

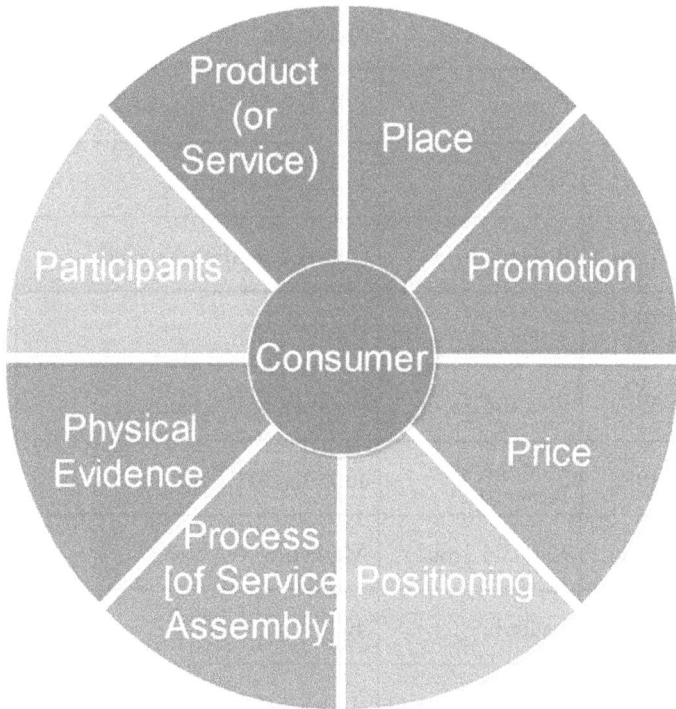

Figure 4 - McCarthy, Trout, Ries, Booms and Bitner 8Ps

Year	Author(s)	Key Point
1561	Calvin	Use of word 'marketing'
1948	Culliton	'Mixer of Ingredients'
1949	Borden	Marketing Mix
1956	Frey	Effective Marketing Mix
1960	McCarthy	Marketing Mix 4Ps
1964	Borden	Concept of Marketing Mix
1969	Trout	Positioning
1972	Ries and Trout	Positioning Era Cometh
1981	Booms and Bitner	additional 3Ps
1986	Ries and Trout	Marketing Warfare
1990	Lauterborn	4Cs
2000 on	various	As, Cs, Os, Vs
2022	Darnton	What customers want

Table 1 - Early Marketing Mix Evolution

Chapter 7

Full Circle

Full Circle Back to Borden, Culliton and Pre-Culliton

What all the various attempts to codify marketing mix since the days of McCarthy have demonstrated, is that when unpacking all the possible ideas for marketing mix elements, there are many possible ingredients.

Almost all the marketing mix variants have the final consumer as the focus of marketing mix (one notable exception being Shimizu who has the corporation as his central focus). That should not come as any surprise when recognizing that ultimately, for most writers, the purpose of marketing is to aid selling products, services, or ideas to end consumers. That is because most writers about marketing mix use a customer-oriented approach. As will be seen in the last two chapters of this book when discussing the relationship between marketing and information warfare, a different approach, competitor-oriented, may be more appropriate these days than a customer-centric approach. The approach may be complicated by having to pass through intermediate customers who are along the supply chain between producers and end consumers.

The first constant feature is the need for focus on the

final consumer, or competitors. The long-term survival of the producer of goods, services or ideas is doomed if the producer loses sight of the wants and needs of the final consumer, or fails to deal with competitors in the marketing mix. The second constant feature is that when constructing a marketing mix there is likely to be a considerable variety of marketing mix elements that can be used.

Thus, we return to the key point made by Culliton – the marketing manager is a 'mixer of ingredients'.

When constructing a marketing mix, put yourself in the shoes of the ultimate consumer of your goods, services, or ideas (not losing sight of any intermediaries in the supply chain).

Marketing Mix example - Smart-phones

If your product is a modern smart phone, what features are important to your buyers? Maybe battery life, usability, security, fashion, and design? If, after you have done some research, those elements prove to be the most important for a majority of customers, then make those the elements of your marketing mix – Battery Life, Usability, Security, Fashion, Design – those are not Ps, Cs, Vs, As, Os, etc. The marketing mix elements identify what is important for the customer. In addition, you will probably need Product (which applies to service, or idea also).

To these customer -oriented marketing mix elements, must be added another element - competitors. Dealing with competitors may be much more important than dealing with customer wants and needs. From a company perspective, it is not the customer wants and needs that are the most significant issues; it is likely to be competitor activity that causes the greatest difficulties.

Marketing Mix examples - Illegal Industries Products and Services

The issue of a customer-oriented marketing mix starting with customer wants and needs can be illustrated by using as examples, some undergraduate work that involved suggesting marketing mixes.

The context was an undergraduate course about global trade. The students were required to select a company or industry as a focus for their work.

The course had raised the issue that when looking at global trade, it should not be thought of as only consisting of the activities of legitimate corporations and trading entities; there are several multi-billion dollar industries involved in illegal or mixed legal and illegal activities such as gambling, drugs, sex, people trafficking, counterfeiting, trade in endangered species, and so forth.

Most students selected an established company, but some selected the drugs, sex, trafficking and counterfeiting industries. All these industries involve the provision of goods or services. The students were encouraged to put themselves 'in the shoes of the buyers' to determine what was important for the buyers, and hence identify candidate marketing mix elements acting as 'mixers of ingredients'.

When looking at prostitution and escorting, some candidate marketing mix elements were health, appearance, obedience, and sustainability (Korpe, 2016).

Marketing mix elements for child trafficking were similar; health, obedience, sustainability, accessibility, value (Landsverk, 2016).

For modern slavery, candidate marketing mix elements are promotion (including via the dark web), customer wants (complex, as motives for acquiring a slave are varied, such as for sex, cheap labour, or organ transplant), reliability, customer value, venue (including online 'red rooms') (Heller, 2016).

For prostitution, marketing mix candidate elements were price, appearance, range of services willing to provide, accessibility, and convenience to buy (von Rueti, 2016).

For ethical research reasons, none of these examples of marketing mixes for illegal or mixed legal-illegal industries was established by primary data obtained from buyers, but was very well supported by a wide range of independent secondary sources. Of course, a fully developed marketing mix would have many more elements than those suggested in these examples. However, in practical classroom and term paper situations, the list of candidate marketing mix elements will, necessarily, be limited. One of the most obvious marketing mix elements missing from these examples is to analyze and deal with the competitive environment.

Chapter 8

Marketing Mix for Ideas

Introductory Comments

In the early days of marketing mix, the initial focus was on marketing products. It was not long before that was extended services. Most marketing efforts are directed to support selling products and services.

As discussed earlier, a common problem arising from student work and some textbooks is frequent attempts to create a marketing mix for a company. This does not work because many organizations selling products actually sell many different products. Even those who interpret marketing mix as 4Ps should see that product is an essential component. Where appropriate, Product should be replaced by Service

One of the most common companies selected by students for producing a marketing mix is McDonald's. Anyone who has visited the McDonald's will know that several products are for sale. Therefore, it makes no sense to create a marketing mix for McDonald's. It may make sense to create a marketing mix for what is perhaps their most common product, a burger. However, great care must be taken because there are many kinds of burger. Another dimension of complexity can be the companies that are trading globally; they may produce variants of products for local markets. For McDonald's, there are burger variants for people with different eating principles such as vegetarians and vegans. Similarly, although beefburgers may be the most common product in the USA, there are other countries that would not accept beefburgers. For example, in India beefburgers are prohibited for Hindus.

As discussed earlier, one aspect of marketing strategy which can be used for a company rather than a product or service is positioning.

Positioning is concerned with how customers and users place companies and their products and services in the consumers' minds.

When someone wants to buy a product or service, they have an idea in their mind of what they want or need. That must be matched to suppliers known to the consumer. There is a lot of literature available about customer product selection but that topic is really beyond the scope of this book.

The key point is that before purchasing a product or service, the idea of doing so must be in the mind of the consumer. How that idea of purchasing a product or service reaches the mind of the consumer is another complex issue.

This discussion so far has been focused on ideas about products and services. However, there are related issues such as pure ideas that are not related to particular products and services but are focused more on someone's belief system.

Considerable effort is expended by many people trying to influence the belief systems of others. There is therefore, overlap between marketing and information warfare. That relationship is explored further in the next chapter.

Indeed, the earliest use of the word marketing discussed above in relation to Calvin (1561), was not concerned with product or service; it was concerned purely with ideas. Therefore this earliest use of 'marketing' is focused entirely on the promotion of ideas (see Appendix B).

As considerable marketing effort is expended on changing what people believe about companies, products, and services, it is important to consider marketing mix for ideas.

The marketing mix for ideas is discussed in the remainder of this chapter and refers to the following marketing mix elements:

- Idea
- Belief
- Promoter
- Epidemiology
- Strategy
- Operations
- Vectors

Idea

The first element of marketing mix for ideas must be one more ideas the promoter would like to be believed by others.

An example of an idea is "vaccination against coronavirus".

Belief

The next element in an idea marketing mix is the belief or beliefs desired in the minds of the recipients.

Taking the example idea of vaccination against

coronavirus, some promoters of the idea will try to convey a belief that vaccinating against coronavirus is an excellent idea and people should do it. There will be others would like recipients of the idea to believe the opposite.

Promoter

The promoter of an idea and belief about that idea is the person who would like to achieve certain beliefs about the idea in the target recipients.

For example, the World Health Organisation along with the national health organizations in many countries want to promote the idea and belief that people should be vaccinated against coronavirus.

There are others who would like to promote the opposite idea and belief that it is not a good idea to be vaccinated against the coronavirus.

Giving examples of organizations that promote ideas and beliefs is symbolic only. Technically, doing so is anthropomorphic and a full detailed analysis would require identifying the specific people within the organization who are promoting the ideas and beliefs.

Epidemiology

Epidemiology is used primarily as the study or science of the spread of diseases. See Bailey (1957) for a discussion of the mathematical theory of epidemics.

By analogy, epidemiology can be used also to study the spread of ideas or fashions within a population.

Some of the analogies between diseases and ideas which are useful include: people within the target population have varying degrees of susceptibility to the disease or idea; some within the population will be resistant to disease or idea.

Different promoters of ideas and beliefs are concerned with increasing susceptibility or immunity within the target population, of particular beliefs and ideas. This issue steps right into the role of ideology, which is the study or science of ideas. Further discussion of these concepts can be found in Darnton (2008).

Strategy

In this marketing mix for ideas, the term strategy is being used in a rather strict way. Strategy is not being used to refer to objectives, which are the ideas and beliefs, but is being used to refer to "how" will the ideas and beliefs be promoted to achieve the promoter objectives?

When formulating strategy, it is the author's view that it is very helpful to separate "what" (objectives) from "how" (strategy)

Operations

Information operations are an integral part of information warfare. When a decision has been taken to conduct information warfare against a population it is usual that information operations are established to conduct that information warfare. Information warfare is usually a shorter intense effort to change ideas and beliefs in a target population. For a more detailed discussion of information operations, see Armistead (2010).

It is very common that when senior leaders of a

a country decides to embark on military operations, people within the government will conduct information operations on their own population with the aim of securing greater acceptance of the proposed military operations, within the population.

This topic is discussed further in the chapter which looks at the relationship between marketing and information warfare.

Vectors

Vectors refer to the various media that can be used to promote ideas and beliefs, or to conduct information operations.

Common vectors include media such as: newspaper advertising: TV and radio advertising; billboards; all other forms of advertising; social media; influencers; and all other channels available to reach target members of a population.

Chapter 9

Marketing Mix for Competition

Background

University research that led to the development of the idea of marketing mix was focused from the 1920s on identifying what elements are needed for effective marketing.

In those early days, marketing can be characterised as production-oriented. Around the time of McCarthy, the approach to marketing became customer-oriented. Ries and Trout introduced positioning and then extended their discussion of marketing warfare for which they pointed out that the key focus of marketing has shifted to be competitor-oriented (for companies involved in competitive markets the key problem has shifted from being customer wants and needs to what the competitors are doing). Therefore, when constructing a marketing mix, it is necessary to deal with competition and competitors. There is plenty of marketing literature available discussing competitive advantage.

Competition Marketing Mix

Fortunately, there are tools readily available that can assist with the development of marketing mix elements that can help dealing with competition.

The key marketing mix elements needed, include:
- Competitors
- Threats
- Strategy

Competitors

These include obvious sources of competition such as other suppliers, but be careful to keep in mind that significant competition can also arise from new disruptive technologies.

Threats

Include in the competition marketing mix elements for all identified threats. Top-level management is often focused more on dealing with the external world than middle management who focus on the operations of the company.

Strategy

Porter's 5-forces model provides several ideas for elements to include. The authors preferred choice is to use the TOWS model by Weihrich (1982).

Identify from that paper by Weihrich what is a TOWS matrix. Create one. The columns are for strengths and weaknesses, and the rows for opportunities and threats. Strategies going into the matrix cells (SO, WO, ST, WT) and overall strategies go into the top left cell.

For a simple real example of a TOWS analysis, see Darnton (2012; pp 74-76).

Chapter 10

Marketing and Information Warfare

Relating Marketing and Information Warfare

This book is about marketing mix; it is not primarily about information warfare. Therefore, the discussion of information warfare will be minimal.

From the discussions in earlier chapters, it should be obvious that one thing in common between marketing and information warfare is that both are concerned with affecting the minds of others.

The closest most texts about marketing get to this position is when they talk about positioning.

The originators of the concept of positioning in marketing, Ries and Trout, come very close to relating marketing and warfare in their book entitled *Marketing Warfare* (1986).

Ries, Trout, and Warfare

Ries and Trout started their contribution to marketing by realizing that a key function of marketing is to affect the minds of potential consumers and customers to the point that a decision is taken to purchase a product or service after having been influenced directly or indirectly by a supplier.

It did not take long for them to consider the possibility that marketing could be seen as a form of warfare albeit focused only on influencing the minds of potential customers, and not involving any form of kinetic warfare.

Ries and Trout found out in one way or another, either by prior knowledge or research, that one of the most famous books about warfare was the 1831/2 book entitled *On War* by Karl von Clausewitz.

Ries and Trout's 1986 book follows von Clausewitz's by analogy for the whole of their book. As they were writing in 1986, the field of information warfare had not yet emerged.

von Clausewitz was concerned primarily with kinetic warfare so the analogies with marketing are awkward. In this sense, Ries and Trout do not make a link between marketing and information warfare.

The analogies found useful in von Clausewitz are focused on strategy and tactics.

They present an important critique of some key writers about marketing, such as Kotler and McCarthy, who Ries and Trout say are focused on what they call the "wants and needs" focus of marketing. Thus, much traditional marketing is focused on meeting the wants and needs of customers by supplying appropriate products and services. They dispute quite vociferously that this is the real essence of marketing. They point out that a very successful vehicle in the USA is the Jeep but it is highly unlikely that focus groups set up to identify customer wants and needs from a vehicle would have specified something like a Jeep.

Ries and Trout paint a picture of the evolution of marketing starting from being production-oriented through being customer-oriented, to today's focus of being competitor-oriented. They point out that these days, the key problems faced by companies are not customer wants and needs; it is what the companies' competitors are doing.

With the availability of big data processing, the marketing mantra of "know your markets" was able to evolve into "know your customers". Big data has not yet evolved to support a new marketing mantra of "know your competitors". The emerging technology of artificial intelligence may be able to help with this problem. Porter's five forces model can also help here.

Hence, the characterization of marketing as dealing with warfare between competitors is understandable. The key link with information warfare is that a major component of the battle space is information. Of course, it is not only information as it can include other factors such as physical location (convenience).

This debate is critical when constructing a marketing mix. In the earlier discussion about McCarthy, the central segment of Customer and Company Objectives should be replaced by Competitors. Marketing mix must include a discussion of how to deal with competitors.

Information Warfare

Information warfare, has only emerged in the late 20th/early21st-centuries as an independent scholarly field. There are suggestions taking its origins back to the 18th and 19th centuries (Bastian, 2019) and there are earlier works about propaganda.

A fundamental aspect of information warfare is that it sets up information as a separate battlefield. One of its objects is the same as the objectives of positioning:

influencing the ideas and beliefs held by the target population. In this sense, marketing and information warfare can be seen as synonymous.

The battlefields of information warfare include information space, cyberspace, and ICT more generally. It is targeted at the ideas and beliefs held by people or equipment used for processing information. It can include trying to reinforce or change ideas and beliefs or to provide disinformation so people will believe things that are not true. In a marketing sense, information warfare is used in the battles against competitors and to manipulate the beliefs of customers and users, or influence positioning.

Those who seek more information about information warfare could access the *Journal of Information Warfare* and books such as Dwivedi (2019) and the collection of readings in Whyte, Thrall, and Mazanec (2020).

In the sense of this book about marketing mix, marketing can be seen as a branch of information warfare. There are plans for a new book about this relationship.

Chapter 11

Green Marketing Mix

Background

So far, it is reasonable to say no generally agreed green marketing mix has yet emerged. It is a topic still in development and will be some time yet before anything can emerge with the certainty of McCarthy's 4Ps.

Since the 1960s, there has been a growing awareness that humanity is facing increasing problems because of resource limitations and effects of human activity such as global warming. These are increasingly serious problems.

As a result, new terms are emerging such as sustainability, corporate social responsibility (CSR) and green washing. Even international law has been evolving to recognise phenomena such as ecocide to be crimes against humanity.

These developments over the past 70+ years are increasingly having an effect on practices such as creating a marketing mix to ensure that all the elements of the marketing mix along with strategies to implement the marketing mix, are as "green" as possible

Therefore, this chapter sets out a range of issues that need to be taken into account when creating a marketing mix in order to go as far as possible towards creating a green marketing mix.

Humanity has experienced resource limitations for

millennia. The production of food has always limited population growth and it is primarily technology that has been used to push out the boundaries of resource availability and use.

An early contributor to the debate about sustainability was Malthus in the 18th century. Interestingly, he was an early founder of what has become the Royal Statistical Society in the UK.

In academic terms, concerns about sustainability of the planet were related to the evolution of systems theory. This culmination of that early thinking which was key in triggering the global debate about global sustainability was the Club of Rome's seminal work entitled *The Limits to Growth* (Meadows et al., 1972).

For a more detailed discussion of the evolution of concerns about sustainability and green washing see the mixed conceptual and empirical paper by Saha and Darnton (2005).

There is another mixed conceptual and empirical paper that readers may find helpful in understanding factors involved in developing a green marketing mix strategy. The empirical part of the paper concludes:

> "The results indicated that environmental orientation has no positively influence on enhancing firm's competitive advantage, but it has positive and significantly effect to the implementation of green marketing mix strategy."
> (Rahmawati, Hadiwidjojo, and Solimun, 2014; p6)

Green Marketing Mix Issues

When constructing a green marketing mix or for the purposes of "greening" in marketing mix, here are some of the issues you need to work on to make the marketing mix greener.

Of course, having developed your green marketing mix it is necessary to develop your green marketing mix strategy for implementation:
- Sustainability
- Environmental Impact
- Corporate Social Responsibility Goals
- Image
- Greenwashing Risks
- Strategies

Sustainability

A key question to answer when discussing sustainability is "what is it that is to be sustained?". It is important to identify sustainability objectives in practical implementable terms and this means identifying target of sustainability. It is also important to identify that what it is to be sustained is consistent with a green marketing mix. As well as identifying what is to be sustained it is necessary to think about the period of time involved.

A useful benchmark that can be used is to check sustainability goals from the marketing mix against the UN Sustainable Development Goals.

Environmental Impact

A marketing mix is focused on some combination of products, services, ideas, and dealing with a competitive environment. Evaluate the likely environmental impact of any of these, and adjust where necessary.

Corporate Social Responsibility Goals

These days, many marketing mixes are being developed within a context of an organization that claims socially responsible conduct.

Understand the CSR goals. These may be internal goals (such as working conditions, employee relations, management style...) or external goals (such as environmental performance, relations and treatment of stakeholders, positioning...).

Try to include performance criteria by which performance against the goals can be measured.

Image

Image merges with positioning. However, it may not be as deep as positioning and is concerned initially with the image of the organization to be created by the green marketing mix.

Greenwashing Risks

There are words and there are deeds. A risk of green washing arises when a difference between words and deeds is detected.

When describing a green washing risk it is important to decide how confidence can be maintained that the organization does what it says in its green marketing mix.

Strategies

Repeating the point that strategies are about "how" things are to be achieved rather than "what" is to be achieved.

Chapter 12

Conclusions and Recommendations

Concluding Comments

This book has travelled a journey including the period from the early 20th century, through many ideas about marketing mix, and back to the thinking of the early writers. It is now 100 years since the beginning of research to try and find the activities and costs involved in bringing products and services to market.

The focus of marketing has evolved from being production-oriented, through being customer-oriented, to being competitor-oriented.

Marketing mix started by being developed for products, extended to services, then extended further to include ideas.

The continued uncritical and bland use of McCarthy's 4Ps should be considered as unacceptable academic work these days. Some of the early work of writers about marketing mix is now very difficult to find, and increasingly so because so many universities are throwing out copies of those early works. Oppressive copyright laws prevent the simple reproduction of works that are very difficult to find, out of print, or published by obscure or failed sources. However, there is plenty of material available to teachers, text book writers, and students to be able to write some good critical commentary when required.

Therefore, there are some recommendations that come from this book::

Recommendation

1. Reject uncritical simplistic marketing mixes based on McCarthy's 4Ps, or the 7Ps when the suggestions of Booms and Bitner are included – but note that the value of all those Ps is important, and after appropriate discussion and considerations, those 4Ps or 7Ps may work for a particular context;

2. Reject marketing mixes created for companies; it only makes sense to create a marketing mix for a particular product, service, or idea (of course, variants of a product, service, or idea may need to be discussed);

3. The extensive literature that has evolved over the last 100 years or so has reconfirmed the situation before 1948, that there is a considerable variety of matters to consider when constructing a marketing plan or marketing mix;

4. Given the fundamental reasons for marketing, always consider including positioning (Ries and Trout) as one of your marketing mix elements (and note that positioning can be applied to a company or brand, unlike marketing mix, which in the absence of very careful reasoning, should only be applied to a product, service or idea, not a company);

5. When constructing a marketing mix, always consider what is particularly important for the buyer (consumer, customer…);

6. Include in your marketing mix all those elements important for the buyer;

7. Include in your marketing mix all those elements important for dealing with competitors;

8. Where relevant, adjust all your marketing mix elements to support a green marketing mix strategy.

Check List of Marketing Considerations

1. Consumers and Uncontrollable Considerations

A. The Nature of the Market

Number of potential buyers–by region. Number of buyers–by region.

Characteristics of buyers–age, income, occupation, education, sex, size of family, color, race–by region.

Characteristics of users, if buyers and users are different–by region.

Where buyers and users live–region, city size, urban and suburban.

Where buyers buy–urban, suburban, rural; trading center, local; type of store.

Size of purchase.

When buyers buy–time of week, time of month, time of year; frequency of purchase.

How buyers buy–brand specification or not; impulse or planned; personal inspection at counter; cash or credit.

Why buyers buy–attitudes, motivation.

Who influences buying decisions–type of product and brand.

Uses for product—primary and secondary.

Broad classes of buyers–race, wage earners, farmers, executives, etc. Attitudes of buyers of type of product by non-buyers of this brand.

Unfavorable attitudes of buyers of brand.

Indications of changes in buying habits.

B. The Structure of the Market
Number of competitors.

Number of brands–national, regional, local.

Share of market by brands, total, regional, city size, type of store.

Characteristics of leading brands. Differentiation of own brand from leaders.

Policies, the offer, methods and tools of principal competitors.

2. Product

A. The Product
Quality–materials, workmanship, design, method of manufacture.

Models and sizes. Essential or luxury. Convenience or shopping.

B. The Package
Attributes of protection, convenience, attractiveness, identification, adaptability to type of retail

outlet, and economy, through:

Material Label-design, color, copy

Size Closure

Shape   Competitive value Construction

C. The Brand
Adequacy with reference to memory value suggestiveness, pleasingness, family expansion, legal protection, goodwill value.

D. Service–Kind, Quantity and Quality.
Installation.
Education in use.
Repair.
Provision of accessory equipment. Delivery.
Credit.
Returned goods.

3. Place

A. Distribution Channels
Total number of retailers, each type by region. Total number of wholesalers, each type by region.

Per cent retailers, each type, handling brand by region.

Degree of aggressive retailer cooperation, by region, store type and city size. Indications of shift in relative importance of channels

4.   Promotion

A. Personal selling
Recruiting and selection methods. Training procedures.

Supervision procedures.

Stimulation devices.

Compensation plan.

B. Advertising
Size of space and time units-effectiveness.

Appeals and themes–effectiveness.

Use of black and white and color-effectiveness.

Methods of merchandising, advertising.

C. Sale Promotion
Types of activity–deal, premiums, bulletins, portfolios, and so on. Cooperative advertising arrangements.
D. Publicity
Volume and nature–releases, clippings. mentions.

5. Price

At factory.

To wholesalers, by type, size and region To retailers, by type, size and regions. Discounts–functional, quantity, cash, other. Allowances and deals.

Service charges.

Price maintenance.

Notes about McCarthy's Adaptation

Adapted by McCarthy (1960; pp 52-54) from: Frey, (1956).

When making this adaptation, McCarthy made some changes, so it is not exactly the same as the list provided by Frey (1956; pp5-9). The changes range from 'political correctness' (he changed 'negro' to 'race'), leaving out some of Frey's material (e.g. Estimated Results for the Current Year), to repositioning and reclassifying some items (e.g. calling Frey's 'Competition, 'The Structure of the Market'), and perhaps most seriously, restructuring several of Frey's other sections into McCarthy's 4Ps: Product, Place, Promotion, and Price.

Reading McCarthy's original book (1960), one could be forgiven for thinking that McCarthy is saying it was Frey who came up with the 4Ps - the reality on checking the originals was that it was more like McCarthy presenting Frey's work in McCarthy's image!

Therefore it is reasonable to conclude that McCarthy was certainly not the originator of the term 'marketing mix', but he seems to be the originator of restructuring the marketing work of others into his 4Ps.

Facsimile of 16th Century 'Marketing'

Calvin-Norton Manuscript

Many readers are likely to appreciate sight of the earliest 16th century source for the term 'marketing'. Here is the section of the page containing 'markettings' (Norton, 1574; book 4 chapter 18, para. 18) based on Calvin, 1561.

To Saluation.

Queene Helene the Grecian Harlot, cause of the vvar of Troy.

great rage, so great furiousnes, so great crueltye: and a Helene in deed, to whom thei so defile themselues with spiritual whoredom, which is the most cursed of al. I do not here so much as once touche with mi litle finger those grosse abuses, wherw thei might color the vnholy purenes of their holy Masse: how filthy markettings thei vse, how vnhonest gaynes thei make w their massings, with how great rauening they fil their couetousnes. Only I do point vnto, & that with few and playn wordes, what maner of thing is euen the very holiest holines of the Masse, for which it hath deserued in

distributed once receiu stan that th Christ. Be other sacra ther ought knowledg thing that raise & set easili vnde hath ben h clared, y is of god to t trust vs o eye to vs h

References

Editorial Note about referencing: This list of references uses a variant of Author-Date referencing. Where available, first names are given in full because of possible cases of multiple authors with the same family name and initials; where there are more than two authors, names are separated by semi-colons (;) to avoid awkward "." or ambiguity introduced by using only comma separators.

******

Allison, S. (2012). "The marketing mix: from products to life enhancing experiences". *Academy of Marketing Annual Conference*, Southampton Management School, University of Southampton, 2-5 July 2012. In: Proceedings of the Academy of Marketing Annual Conference, Southampton: Southampton Management School, University of Southampton.

Armistead, Leigh (2010) *Information Operations Matters: Best Practices* . Lincoln, NE: Potomac Books, Inc University of Nebraska Press.

Bailey, N.T.J., (1957), *The Mathematical Theory of Epidemics*, London: Charles Griffin & Co. Ltd.

Bastian, Nathaniel D. (2019) "Information Warfare and Its 18th and 19th Century Roots", The Cyber Defense Review, Fall 2019 pp 31-36. Available at: https://cyberdefensereview.army. mil/CDR-Content/Articles/Article-View/Article/2017786/ information-warfare-and-its-18th-and-19th-century-roots/

Bhatia, Vivek (2010) "Evolving Marketing basics: 4 V's for 4 C's through 4 P's", Markadising Zone, web article available at: http://vivek-markadiser.blogspot. co.uk/2010/03/evolving-marketing-basics-4-vs-for-4-cs.html. [accessed 2016-02-01].

Booms, Bernard H. and Bitner, Mary J. (1981) "Marketing Strategies and Organization Structure for Service Firms" in Donnelly, James H., and George, William R. (eds) *Marketing of Services*, Proceedings of the American Marketing Association's 1981 Special Educators' Conference, Orlando,

62

Florida, February 8-11 1981 pp47-51. Chicago, IL: American Marketing Association.

Borden, Neil H. (1950) *Advertising Text and Cases*, Chicago, Il: Richard D. Irwin, Inc.

Borden, Neil H. (1964) "The Concept of the Marketing Mix". *Journal of Advertising Research*, 4(2) June 1964 pp 2-7, and in Schwartz, George (editor), *Science in Marketing*, New York: John Wiley & Sons, Inc., pp 386-397.

Borden, Neil H. and Marshall, Martin V. (1959) *Advertising Management: Text and Cases*, Homewood, Il: Richard D. Irwin, Inc.

Claycamp, Henry J., and Liddy, Lucien E. (1969) "Prediction of New Product Performance: An Analytical Approach", *Journal of Marketing Research* 6(4) November 1969, pp 414- 420.

Culliton, James W. (1948) *The Management of Marketing Costs*, Boston, MA: Division of Research, Graduate School of Business Administration, Harvard University.

Darnton, Geoffrey (2008) "Religion Ideology, and Information Warfare" *in Proceedings of The 3rd International Conference on Information Warfare and Security* held at the Peter Kiewit Institute, University of Nebraska, Omaha, on 24-25 April 2008 pp 109-116. Reading, UK: Academic Conferences International

Darnton, Geoffrey (2012) Business Process Analysis. Bournemouth: Requirements Analytics.

Darnton, Geoffrey (2017) "Return Marketing Mix to its Origins", *Business and Management Journal* 1(1).

Dennis, Charles; Fennech, Tino; and Merrilees, Bill (2005) "Sale the 7 Cs: teaching/training aid for the (e-)retail mix" *International Journal of Retail and Distribution Management*, 33(3) pp 179-193.

Dwivedi, Anurag (2019) Modern Information Warfare : Operations, Doctrine and Force Structures. Pentagon Press.

Frey, Albert Wesley (1956) *The Effective Marketing Mix: Programming for Optimum Results*, Hanover, NH: Amos Tuck School of Business Administration, Dartmouth College.

Heller, Michelle. (2016) *The Modern Slave Industry*, Undergraduate Student Assignment. Regent's University London.

Korpe, Emma (2016) *Prostitution and Escorting*, Undergraduate Student Assignment. Regent's University London

Kwitny, Johnathan (1972) " 'Positioning' Ads " *Wall Street Journal*, 13th December 1972.

Landsverk, Cecilie (2016) *Human Trafficking of the World's*

63

Children, Undergraduate Student Assignment. Regent's University London.

Lauterborn, R. (1990) "New marketing litany; Four Ps passe; C-words take over", *Advertising Age*, October 1st 1990, p26.

Lawrence, E; Corbitt, B; Tidwell, A; Fisher, J; and, Lawrence, J.R., (1998), *Internet Commerce: Digital Models for Business*, Wiley.

McCarthy, E. Jerome (1960) *Basic Marketing: A Managerial Approach*, Homewood, Il: Richard D. Irwin, Inc.

McCarthy, E. Jerome (1964) *Basic Marketing: A Managerial Approach* (Revised Edition), Homewood, Il: Richard D. Irwin, Inc.

McCarthy, E. Jerome (1968) *Basic Marketing: A Managerial Approach* (3rd Edition), Homewood, Il: Richard D. Irwin, Inc.

McCarthy, E. Jerome and Perreault, William D. Jr. (ed.) (2000) Essentials of Marketing: A Global Managerial Approach. Irwin/McGraw-Hill.

Meadows, Donella H, Meadows, Dennis L. Randers, Jorgen, and Behrens, William W. III (1972) *The Limits to Growth; A Report for the Club of Rome's Project on the Predicament of Mankind.* Potomac Associates.

Midgley, David F. (1977) *Innovation and New Product Marketing*, London: Croom Helm.

Norton, Thomas (1574; 1561) The Institvtion of Christian Religion, vvrytten in Latine by maister Ihon Caluin, and translated into Englysh according to the authors last edition. London: Reinolde Vvolf & Richarde Harisson. A copy of this can be accessed at: http://quod.umich. edu [the page numbers indicated in that source are not convincing when compared against the original book]. This 1574 edition is the same as the 1561 edition, with some re-pagination.

OED (2009) *Oxford English Dictionary* (2nd ed. On CD-ROM Version 4.0), Oxford: Oxford University Press.

Rahmawati, Rina; Hadiwidjojo, Djumilah and Solimun, Noermijati (2014) "Green Marketing Mix As Strategy to Improve Competitive Advantage in Real Estate Developer Companies". International Journal of Business and Management Invention 2 (11) pp 06-12.Ries, Al and Trout, Jack (1972a) "The Positioning Era Cometh" *Advertising Age* (April 24, 1972)

Ries, Al and Trout, Jack (1972b) "Positioning Cuts Through Chaos in Market Place", *Advertising Age* (May 1, 1972)

64

Ries, Al and Trout, Jack (1972c) "How to Position Your Product", *Advertising Age* (May 8, 1972)

Ries, Al and Trout, Jack (1981) *Positioning: The Battle for Your Mind*, New York: McGraw-Hill Book Company

Ries, Al and Trout, Jack (1986) *Marketing Warfare*, New York: McGraw-Hill Book Company

Ries, Al and Trout, Jack (2005) *Marketing Warfare: 20th Anniversary Edition* Authors' Annotated Ed.. McGraw-Hill.

Saha, Monica and Darnton, Geoffrey (2005). "Green companies or green con-panies: are companies really green, or are they pretending to be? *Business and Society Review.* 110 (2): 117-157

Shimizu, Koichi (n.d.) "Professor Koichi Shimizu's 7Cs Compass Model", available at: http://www.josai.ac.jp/~shimizu/essence/Professor%20Koichi%20Shimizu's%207Cs%20Compass%20Model.html [accessed 2015-05-09].

Shostack, G. Lynn (1977a) "Human Evidence: A New Part of the Marketing Mix", *Bank Marketing*, June 1977 pp 32-34.

Shostack, G. Lynn (1977b) "Breaking Free from Product Marketing", *Journal of Marketing* 41, April, pp 73-80.

Trout, Jack (1969) " "Positioning" is a game people play in today's me-too market Place", *Industrial Marketing* Vol 54, No 6 (June 1969).

Trout, Jack with Rivkin, Steve (1996) *The New Positioning: The Latest on the World's #1 Business Strategy*, New York: McGraw-Hill Inc.

von Rueti, Sarah (2016) *The World of Trade in Prostitution*, Undergraduate Student Assignment. Regent's University London.

Weihrich, Heinz (1982) "The TOWS matrix—A tool for situational analysis". Long Range Planning 15(2) pp 54-66.

White, Livingstone (2013) "The Marketing Mix Evolution: From 4P's to 4C's to 4V's and Now… O's and A's?". Website article available at: http://www.livingstonwhite.com/ academic/teaching/the-marketing-mix-evolution-from-4ps-to-4cs-to-4vs-and-now-os- and-as/.

Whyte, Christopher; Thrall, A. Trevor and Mazanec, Brian M. (eds.) (2020) *Information Warfare in the Age of Cyber Conflict*. Routledge.

Index

Symbols

Marketing Mix Notes

Marketing Mix Notes

Marketing Mix Notes   83